T0104616

please don't ask

LYMAN DITSON

BALBOA.
PRESS

A DIVISION OF HAY HOUSE

Balboa Press books may be ordered through booksellers or by contacting:

Balboa Press
A Division of Hay House
1663 Liberty Drive
Bloomington, IN 47403
www.balboapress.com
1 (877) 407-4847

Print information available on the last page.

ISBN: 978-1-5043-5032-7 (sc)
ISBN: 978-1-5043-5033-4 (e)

Library of Congress Control Number: 2016901785

Balboa Press rev. date: 02/12/2016

Contents

please don't ask

please don't ask if tears you see
an open heart breaking free
and drawing lines down my face
not sadness is it I embrace
nor guilt nor pain do I flee

but glorious worlds counting three
filled with life on land and sea
beauty's magic in this place
oh please don't ask

where loving wishes are to be
and roving teachers comfort thee
these of whom our dreamings trace
imagine truth at one's own pace
and grateful tears now touching me
oh please don't ask

dome of green

standing not so high
this tree of greenish dome
reaching out
from a circle of dirt
in a valley
of concrete.
walkers walk
passing this dome of green
unhearing
unseeing
uncaring
of the gift within.
but a young boy stops
as a song of beauty
trilling
from within
the dome of green
touches his heart.
an empty patch
fist-sized
at the back
of the dome of green
to see within
the songster.

the young boy peers
thru nature's window
and beholds
a hollowed dimness
with leafless branches
arranged by God.
upon a perch
regal
in black
with white feather
streaks
a most beautiful bird
singing
a song unique
in all the ages
as walkers walk
passing the dome of green
uncaring.

A Poet's Lament

How, these days, do I spend my time?
arming myself with pen and pad,
scribbling poems that often rhyme,
at times my musings aren't so bad.

some love to read my poetry,
happiness given to those who've read,
I once gave a poem for one to see,
but he said I should be a clerk instead.

!*#!?*

why beat your brains thinking up verse --
about things that people can't understand.
to be a poet is a terrible curse,
upon one's head insults will land!

self

what of this thing —-the self
of birth unremembered
of death the end

sustained by thought and reason
this ghost of nothing
desperate for attention

like an orchestra conductor gone mad
convinced
he is the music

unable to hear
twinkling streams
and flailing leaves

unable to see
everything
everywhere

until a time
when batons
weigh heavy

and the soul of the universe
softly
waits

to be recognized

pride

proud of this kingdom boasts many men,
raise the flag and remember when,
birth of their empire was won in battle,
glory in war runs the prattle,

but truth sees thru a proud man's heart,
tis not love of kingdom for a start,
though that's the words of a puffed up crowd,
it's pride they love, this drug called proud.

folding walls

I wait
for life to open
to a wondrous
garden

no fear
this time
I say to the
silence

just hold me
and sing
to me
softly

until the walls
fold
and everything
is alive

dog nap

there is this tiny, near six pound dog
who sleeps with me when the time gets late
he's being a stubborn mattress hog
there is this tiny, near six pound dog
he's being a stubborn mattress hog
this serious matter of real estate
there is this tiny, near six pound dog
who sleeps with me when the time gets late

carnival

racing hearts
on iron seats
swinging
through the night sky
conjuring delusions

disdainful of calm --
laughter grips laughter
seeking
to escape
all judgment.

papier-mache knights
in contests
drunken
silly heroes
for this instant

as buxom statues
secretly mine
gold
with shy looks
of black circles.

shadowy faces
on stilts of ivory
hiding
their tears
with greasy smiles

while thin drooling suits
hustle and smirk
standing
on plateaus
of rotting wood.

soaring black feathers
caw to the earth
bitching
at wasted clangs
of a circus concocted

and roosters
wedged in wire shells
trancing
on the distant yawps
of insanity

of cackling sirens
with calls to forsake
whispers
of love true,
quiet and gentle.

loneliness reaches
while not letting go
hoping
to quench
a rejected need

as the stars
warn softly ---
grace
is not home
in a carnival.

sparkle

a moment of sparkle
is just a wink
lasting eons --
a creation
of a trillion stars,
as hearts reach
and desires fade
and pass into silence
holding a moment
for the next
sparkle

Noah

Oh tell me Noah, did you cry
for those left standing on the land?
as sheets of rain fell from the sky,
did you weep or bless God's hand?

all the derision you could stand,
teasings and accusations fly,
oh tell me Noah, did you cry
for those left standing on the land?

even though you knew then why
others there were left to strand,
riding waves above them high,
did you feel of justice grand?
oh tell me Noah, did you cry
for those left standing on the land?

stars

I give my heart to the stars
where silence
crushes
my will
pulling me closer to
emptiness

Cricketland

zoom by the seat of your pants
in Cricketland
dream, you Beatle disciples
now found this city of children
you urban shamans
yellow-eyed grackles dart and dive
daredevils
more wiles than the homeless
staking out stops
baking
scientist waiters grumble and groan
as the rush to musicville presses
and bulges
muses, impatient, stand in line
inspiration is no stranger here
in Cricketland
dance you minstrels of the desert
on patios of umbrellas
till clouds boom and crack
and glorious rain finds you bopping
everywhere
to conform is what is feared
in this city that calls itself weird
this pocket of partisans surrounded
by convention
this Cricketland

bold

bold angel prayers from deserts be
talks of peace by children three
stars of love to silence the drum
of vengeance calling out from some
to becloud the hope of light to free

oh gaze across the cosmic sea
all brother's souls are just as we
adoring stars from all we come
bold angel prayers –

and if these children don't agree
caused by a leader who cannot see
by stirring war to make hearts numb
then learn where beauty's fury's from
as nowhere from love can one flee
bold angel prayers –

The General

iron cannonballs slam
into soft columns
of boys slinging broken bodies
across the smoky barren

the charging angry
skip over
these screaming rag-dolls
of grey and blue
as the General surveys

not the hand
of the Almighty

hatred roars
from those on their feet
as frightened sobs call
out from the writhing
in this hell

on this battered glen
sloggy from blood and mud
bayonets gash and twist
midst hurled curses

not driven by the hand
of Magnificence

the General regards
his boys dying to the forefront
and he fights the escape
from his eyes
of a tear

racing slivers of fiery metal
rip and tear the young
who bury fear
in the collective strength
of insanity

not from the hand
of Glory

in the center of madness
on furrowed grime
a baby sparrow
struggles
lost

and a General
trudges onto the field of war
passing the dead
as tiny balls of lead
spray muck all about

not fired by the hand
of God

calloused fingers
pick up this creature so small
placing him gently
in a downy nest
on a young tree's bough
as the carnage hesitates—
...this moment
for the courageous—
...hand of Love

melt

shatter my will
into a million pieces –
and allow me to wish
alongside the wind
batter my reason
into irrelevant drivel –
and ask me how
my heart has opened
cast my knowledge
into infinity's canyons –
and show me love
of simple light
gently pull me
away from myself –
so that I may melt
into beauty eternal

Adam's Excuse

She tried my honor with a triple dog dare,
to pilfer a prize from the apple tree,
I prowled the way for an orb to snare,
she tried my honor with a triple dog dare,
I prowled the way for an orb to snare,
then grabbed the fruit much to her glee,
she tried my honor with a triple dog dare,
to pilfer a prize from the apple tree.

again

galloping horses of beauty
bearing down
on me
from all corners of stillness
yet

tangling thoughts
wrestle me away
from
my liberation
again

prior to eternity

remember when we all could see,
prior to eternity,
we laid in glades on silky dew,
peeked thru branches, jigsaws of blue,
touched close the heart beat of a tree,

we'd skim the surges of the sea,
and swim the skies, stretched and free,
soar thru valleys of greenish hue,
remember when.

slept 'neath the stars, heaven's marquee,
prior to eternity,
brooks' melodies we'd nestle to,
crunchy brown leaves we'd scamper thru,
every breath, an act of beauty,
remember when.

999 Ravens

as the ravens
gather
dipping and spinning
in a concocted whirlpool
in the dimming sky
overhead

these seraphic signs
puzzle
busy walkings
below
dressed
in nervous titters

wonders of wonder
with black pearl eyes
twirling
like a dark spotted
twister
calling out

this cacophony of rhythm
with wings
full
of wind
portending tomorrows
today

as more
feathered magicians
gather
from all horizons
to join the ebon ballet
scripted by the mind of God

Dear Brother

Oh sweet Love, my baby brother,
my precious sibling, like no other,
I join the vigil near bedside,
you've left not yet, yet still I cried,

stories and memories bounce through this room,
as ones who Love you fend off gloom,
remember Beloved when I was a tyke,
and you'd rock and sing night songs I'd like,

I was the one who first fell asleep,
as off to dreamland my mind would sweep,
then child bard, twas your turn to doze,
and blessed silence the night would close,

now with this world, you reach your sunset,
you're Heart is pure, nothing to regret,
Eternal Beauty unimaginal Bliss,
I spoke of this Beauty and gave you a kiss,

and yesterday, your face lit up as a Star,
the step to the Sublime is not very far,
and your Heart so knew, it was told by your eyes,
you knew of this Beauty overhead in the skies.

and soon, when as an Angel you become,
I would ask of you that I yet hear from,
as I am still here, a promise you'll keep,
dear young brother, please sing me to sleep.

frog heaven

twas once upon a time,
off far in a magical place,
traveled a prince in his prime,
an evil witch that he would chase,
they met each other in forest's space,
she promptly changed him to a frog,
abruptly ended the prince's chase,
and he sat bewildered upon a log,
as she disappeared into the fog,

so disappointed he became,
a small green frog was he,
no longer was he of great fame,
no castle home for him to be,
this small blue pond nearby a tree,
from whereby he then glanced around,
and little things that he could see,
subtle treasures he may have found,
from high in the treetops to the ground,

butterflies bright became his friends,
a sparkling of stars for slumbering under,
magical fish in reeds they'd blend,
melodic storms of musical thunder,
chirping jays with songs of wonder,
forest's smells of storied scents,
missed by many, perhaps their blunder,
a secret heaven is where he went,
so grace's bounty to him was leant,

the days, they rolled into the weeks,
causing many months to gallop by,
but the frog had found what everyone seeks,
his precious place under the sky,
many nights in joy would he cry,
for this glorious place now his home,
as thru all time his soul could fly,
no longer was his heart to roam,
but don't yet stop this fateful poem,

a beautiful princess came along,
one bright and sunny day,
singing aloud a radiant song,
to his pond she made her way,
spotted the frog and knew he may –
be a prince who needs a kiss,
maybe then with her he'd stay,
a chance for her so great as this,
leaned in close so not to miss,

sat he stunned as her lips grew near,
he on his favorite lily pad,
suddenly he was frozen with fear,
to leave this pond would make him sad,
a life so grand one might add,
decided with the pond he'd dwell,
truly then he'd still be glad,
he hopped away as fast as hell,
as shrieked the princess as she fell.

clouds

these visions of fluff
temper star rays
while gentle winds mold them
into wisps and giants
who in time
sneak into the darkness
of night
where glowing moon beams
outline the hovering shapes
of these veils of beauty

trying to feel

mother huddled over the picture screen
intense
typing useless words
to feel
more feelings

as baby beside her cries
bundled in
cotton
on an olive green
bench

alone
trying to feel
the warmth
of love
from a mother

lost
trying to find
the warmth
of favor
from a glinting phone

star love

I have a universe
where my experiences have
drawn mountains and rivers
drawn antelope and whales
drawn sorrow and joy
drawn all that is

like a grand superb sketcher
with my universe
with it's truths and untruths
I seek to be loved
and to love
like only the stars can love

that gently reach to me
in the magic places
of my universe
I find
both creator and creation --
this beauty

adobe land

urban prairie dogs
watch beaten pick-ups
full
of rakes and branches
roll by
their town of holes

as the city square
teems
with grannies
playing dress-up
as Annie Oakley
crusted in turquoise

while hidden eateries
with old wooden tables
cruelly
demand the decision
of red or green
immediately

and famished bears
unlawfully beg
ringing doorbells
in the cool pastels
of
this desert of mountains
of this
place of pueblos
of sated painters
this place
called
adobe land

now

all around at once
the amazing now
faster than sound or light
everywhere found
everyone bound
by the amazing
now

Geronimo

Don't hold your tears Geronimo,
call to the clouds and let them flow,
upon your family the ambush swoops,
innocent snuffed by craven troops,
they from a town in Mexico,

bloody vengeance swore by this woe,
all be foes to die by your blow,
compassion lost for any group,
don't hold your tears,

as time goes by, your enemies grow,
as time goes by, your arrows slow,
unto the end, a warrior's whoop,
as an aged body begins to stoop,
don't hold your tears.

to sing

this grand event --
this threshold of light
by cause of
the opening of eyes

passes shortly
to this final affair --
an ending,
this closing of eyes

yet all is not nothing
for between opening and closing
is a chance to sing
a unique song to the eternal

dark factories

I remember what it was like
before
the factories went dark

the joes and toms
with their dull metal
lunch pails
walking from the lot
chuckling
about hank
who slid and fell in the bowling alley
the night before

was so damned funny

then the next day
the joes and toms and hanks stopped
and the factories
became dark

no more clanging
no more buzz drilling
no more whistles

just cracked concrete
and weeds
and big dark
factories

people don't really
look at the dark factories

they've become the background
like broken barns
and rusting tractors
rotting in empty fields

but now
after years have passed
there are dark factories
that humm
and swish
and clang

you can't see inside
because they are dark

no joes or toms

only robots
that need no light
because they have no eyes

screw the dark factories

roving wolf

Oh roving wolf. What's in a day? Pursuit of a swift-footed jackrabbit? Sitting in the sun gathering beams? Singing a song of fables and legends, that hollows the spirit of man? Oh roving wolf. What's in a day?

Lumpy

Made a friend, talked a while,
said some things that brought a smile,
but something said made me jumpy,
she spoke of naked men as lumpy,

the voice inside I chose to hear,
tried to compare me to Richard Gere,
so off to the mirror in search of truth,
reflecting back a handsome youth,

off the clothes, this act so bold,
wow, I looked a little old,
then my middle made me grumpy,
I was in fact a little lumpy,

but a comforting thought I'll bet is true,
Richard Gere is lumpy too.

finally

tell me just
one secret
before my face
melts
into lines and crags
and crowded memories
vanish
in death

teach me how to
touch
life
before I take a last glance
in terror
or peace
and my precious thoughts
mean nothing

let me travel
with timelessness
and
not remember
this relentless
thinker
I call me
finally

winter gifts

each snowflake
by moonbeams
glistens
rolling on the chilled winds
of heaven

sculpted glassy
chips
formed with shiny facets
perfectly
chiseled by frosty airs

these tiny stars
fall to earth
with promises
of life
to wake up beauty

over hill and plain
weaving
blankets of white
these trifling sparkles
from infinity

these unique
blessings
of grace ---
oh these wintry gifts
of angels

The Bracelet

today bestowed
a bracelet
not of gold or silver
adorned
diamond-less with
no sparkling sapphires

today bestowed
a bracelet
so plain
yet she smiled such a big smile
not knowing
this bracelet's value

today bestowed
a bracelet
to mom
whose heart rings simple joy
whose past memories
have far faded

today bestowed
a bracelet
of paper and plastic
held together by a shiny rivet
with the letters DNR --
oh silent sadness

Taught

Peace will shelter when follows the day,
buds of Life are Creator taught,
grasp of Earth's weaves thru flawless play,
not tangled amiss by chaotic thought,

tree-circled meadows, not for distraught,
coy brooks giggle, inviting to stay,
Peace will shelter when follows the day,
buds of Life are Creator taught,

begetters one, show nurturing's way,
with prodding Love, no agenda sought,
ten-thousand mentors, Angels they,
feathers that sparkle, beautifully wrought,
Peace will shelter when follows the day,
buds of Life are Creator taught.

cage

In the cage of self
spinning tales
of woe
and glory
seeking discovery
from others

as if a living
story
could be a jewel
of which
all would desire
to hold

seeking eternity
from the
shifting sands
of
piddling
mortal ends

but then beastly
storms
break apart
one's
unyielding sagas -
to dust

for tempests reveal
the lostness
of narrations -
while preparing
souls
for

a tiny place
where
peace resides
where nothing
is
everything

remember me

my face, my words, my funny way,
dear mom, please remember me,
a wobbly train through skies of grey,
a thousand miles of scenes to see,

smile my name, my hopeful plea,
grasp but a moment on this day,
my face, my words, my funny way,
dear mom, please remember me,

seeking with past times for a ray,
of discovered light to break free,
your eyes can't place me, lost are they,
then a kind stranger, must I be,
my face, my words, my funny way,
dear mom, please remember me.

Captain, Captain

Captain, Captain, can't you tell?
the future holds a storm from hell,
but lost are you amongst this mess,
all you do is stand and guess,

As the leader you think you'll win,
the patience of the sky wears thin,
maybe this time the knight in white,
is a roiling ocean ready for fight.

to write

how can you
show
me the glows of
eternity
and in time
let me forget

led by distraction
and desire
wallowing
lost like a pup
alone
wandering

until I pick up pen
and sketch
symbols
that somehow
open my
heart

and then I see
mountains
of clouds
and hear beauty
calling on
the winds again

Yay!

Oh how they worry
that the air is thinning
Yay! for climate change
It means nature's winning

a basic poem

```
10 CLS /* This will clear screen */
20 for A = 1 to 3 /* This will print 3 blank lines */
30 print ""
40 next A
50 gosub 200
60 gosub 300
70 print ""
80 gosub 400
90 gosub 200
100 print ""
110 gosub 500
120 gosub 600
130 gosub 200
140 end

200 print "oh revelations of eternal grace"
210 print "the splendor of a heartfelt poem"
220 return
300 print "crashing through logic's place"
310 print "in all mansions beauty roams"
320 return
400 print "the soft invite of returning home"
410 print "the rendering to awe's embrace"
420 return
500 print "all numbing thoughts to erase"
510 print "to vanish like a white wave's foam"
520 return
600 print "staring empty at beauty's face"
610 print "no more seeking all alone"
620 return
```

thought

thought
creeps through open doors
like a stealthy fox
with
no home

causing stirring waves
to jostle
crashing
into others lost
this fragile ship

till the quiet heart
hears
the incessant noise
and whispers
"not I"

Just a Trash Can

I stood and stared at an old trash can
standing alone and grey aside a curb
hobbling past on cane a man
in time many passed without a word

"no one to myself will glance
unless they drop trash...
just perchance."

stunned I was that this object here
uttered a voice I plainly heard
it sounded it's feelings loud and clear
this garbage bin had the gift of word!

"all alone am I bolted down strong
looked at with disdain like I...
don't belong."

madness I believed I had wrought
a talking trash can I can't believe
from too much work, too much thought
gone too far, myself to deceive

"paper, wires, goop, flossing strings
cans, bottles, food, some...
grossly things."

people passing by decidedly near
to and fro without a care
so obvious that they couldn't hear
just I alone this cross to bear

"with my odor they disagree
they pull their children away...
from me."

now it tells me about it's smell
so many trash cans in this city
I believe I'm in trash can hell
a metal bin wants my pity!

"happy to see me, some look up
as long as it takes to toss me...
their cup."

what shall I do? run away?
over to the nearest liquor store
but who knows what the sidewalk will say
or maybe the counter or even the door

"why not drop some perfume in
or paint velvet flowers all over...
my bin."

as I stand midst this passing crowd
I now understand this spectacle
it's God speaking to me very loud
from a garbage filled receptacle

"once an old man in torn up clothes
stopped with his cart, it was I...
he chose."

Moses had his burning bush
Mohammed had his secret cave
Buddha alone sitting on his tush
but look to me what God has gave!

"with my contents he had no revile
he searched thru me with the...
greatest smile!"

no, it's nonsense that God would speak
to anyone from a grey trash can
I know who it is my soul they seek
it's got to be from that pesky Satan

"to the old man I was a vast gold mine
with crusted rubies and...
sapphires fine!"

none of these theories seem right somehow
this nonsense is going way to far
maybe I should just end it now
and throw myself at a moving car

"this old man to me seemed shrewd
not just a cupcake who...
comes unglued."

there's no doubt about this very thing
I know I'm having a brain attack
but one thing's true, softens the sting
at least I've spoken nothing back

with love

to be lifted to eternity
and gently set down
with love
in this bustle
somewhere the taste lingers
like the sweetest plum
with love
now amongst madness
fading vision fans fear's flame
of mayhaps staying
with love
in the mundane
take me again my heart beseeches
lift the veil yet again
with love
in this blindness
touchless still I wait
and labor
with love
to lose myself
lift me again my mind cries out
as my heart confuses
with love
for eternity's embrace

Mount Olympus

lights…camera…action!

buy the rag, reading is fine,
paparazzi does his tricks,
blurry photos on page nine,
how'd he get those close-up pics?

goddesses, gods, what a thrill,
drama of humans it seems,
oh to be on Olympus hill,
and behold the reckless schemes,

Venus gal causes a war,
Hera is jealous again,
Pluto is dating a whore,
and Zeus is having a yen,

legends of the silver screen,
those souls the world exalts,
naked are the king and queen,
all this love of human faults.

the rising waves

where, now all, do we take our fight?
on whom do we declare our war?
'gainst God's designs are we to smite --
the rising waves upon each shore

the winds our foe, on this we swore,
and cursed the clouds hanging white,
where, now all, do we take our fight?
on whom do we declare our war?

worlds awaken to their plight,
pressing forward, a thunderous roar,
the mountains stir, blocking light,
screaming gusts where ravens soar,
where, now all, do we take our fight?
on whom do we declare our war?

a napping dove

scattered billboards
grant soundless promises
to lure
as perched atop
a crying dove
looking over this place of concrete
and glass
filled with flitterings
like a carnival
trapped.
wires as branches
line the painted concrete
trails
under rolling plastic monsters
humming
as protesting horns mingle
with angelic sirens
to bring order
to those
chasing soundless promises
windows dot columns of brick
as they who cannot see doves
scurry about
on their hurried quest
for immortality

while a crying dove
perched atop a silent billboard
naps
only to join again
dreams
of yesterday– when crying doves sung
ringing over breezy treetops
until the moon would find them
napping
with dreams of tomorrow.

Wizardry

to a waddling wizard
from a cavern of
concoctions --
what words would you
brave?

would requests of
riches call to his
compassion --
like the cries
of a baby bird?

or maybe to
dare him
to change stones to gold
that one might gather
graciously.

or could he,
like a generous Genie
captured,
humbled --
award three wishes?

no.. perhaps this
wily wizard,
this bearded bard,
would gift to you........
simply....

the poverty of a poem.

ending

when sings the fat lady
at the end of a time
where knowing tramples
on the beauty of all

so swift the movements
of smoothing
the flaws
of creation

for by chance
seems
the measured chaos
of removal

as man cries out
"what have we done!"
to the stars
where patience has left

and by his own crafted
weapons
removes
himself

sparrows never die

the flutter of a sparrow
like the shimmering
leaves
of a windswept elm
display their calling
with no debate
like the moon
lifting salty waves
and when the soul
of a sparrow
knows it cries
a final cry —
angels
in gleaming chariots of love
gently gather
beauty

touch

and when you sing to me,
sing from the heart,
for I have heard angels...

and when you dance with me,
dance with great joy,
for I have seen bliss...

and when you speak to me,
speak with pure love,
for I have known beauty...

and when you touch me,
touch me with care...
for I am in heaven

Printed in the United States
By Bookmasters